Grazing and Agrestic Customs of the Outer Hebrides

OUTER HEBRIDES

BY

ALEXANDER CARMICHAEL

Printed for the Benefit of the Crofter Royal Commission.

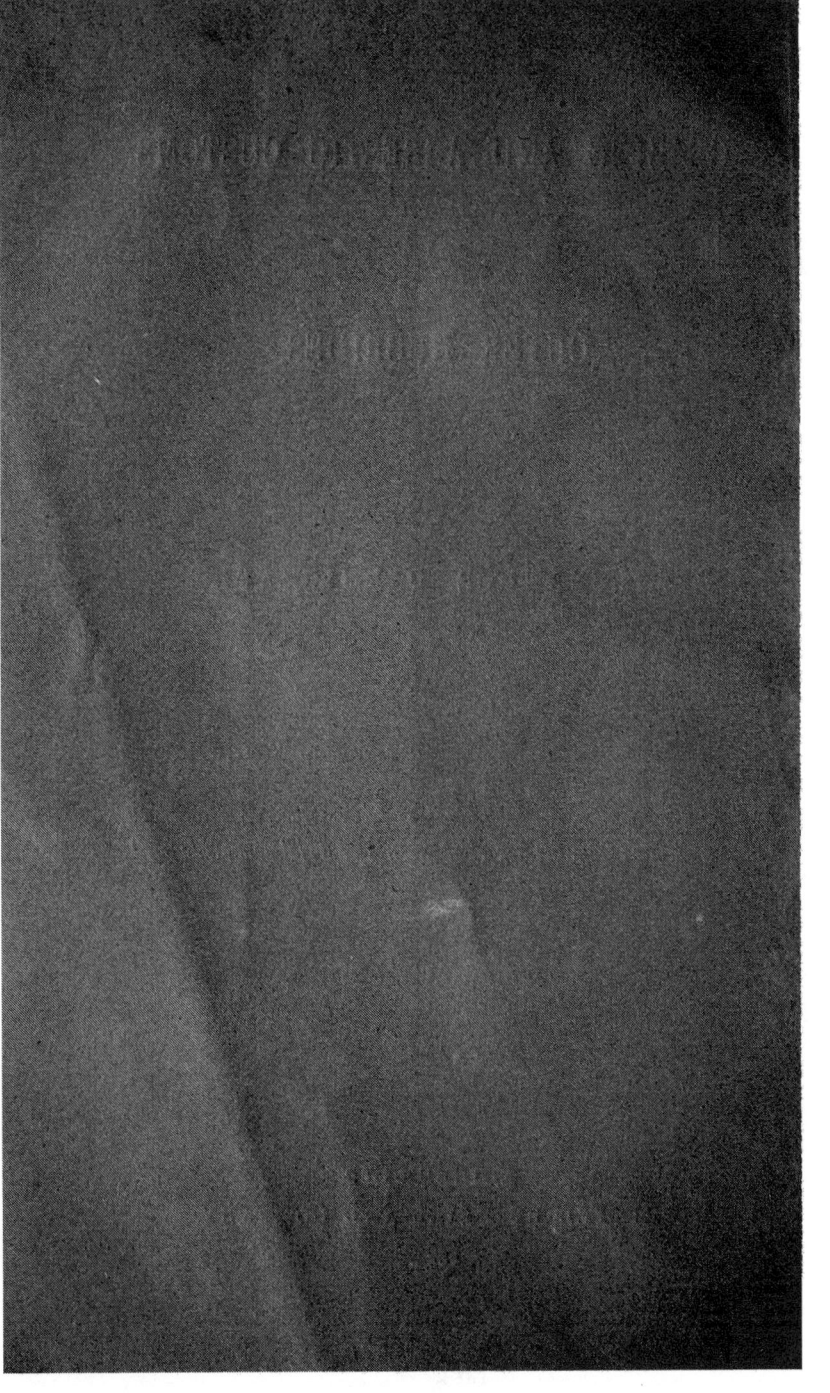

*For the acceptance of Sir Toi Ratos C.f.
with the warm admiration of the writer,*

GRAZING AND AGRESTIC CUSTOMS

*Good Friday
1885*

OUTER HEBRIDES.

BY

ALEXANDER CARMICHAEL.

Reprinted from the Report of the Crofter Royal Commission.

EDINBURGH:

PRINTED BY NEILL AND COMPANY.

1884.

NOTE.

This paper was written at the request of Lord Napier and Ettrick for the Crofter Royal Commission, over which his Lordship presided. Government have courteously granted the writer permission to reprint a few copies to give to his friends.

Originally the paper was meant to contain some account of the Geological changes, and of the Natural History and Antiquities of the Outer Hebrides, but these not coming within the scope of the Commission, Lord Napier found himself obliged to exclude them.

The paper is hurried and fragmentary, and contains but little of what might have been said of the interesting people and customs of the Western Isles.

"The account of the old customs is the most interesting thing in your Report; the old hymns are charming."—*Extract of Letter from a Nobleman in London to Lord Napier.*

ALEXANDER CARMICHAEL.

31 RAEBURN PLACE, EDINBURGH,
14th *July* 1884.

XCIX.

GRAZING and AGRESTIC CUSTOMS of the Outer Hebrides, by
ALEXANDER CARMICHAEL

GEOGRAPHICAL

The Long Island comprehends a series of islands 116 miles in length. The breadth varies from one mile to twenty-six miles.

In shape the Long Island resembles an artificial kite—Lews being the body, and the disarticulated tail trending southward and terminating in Bearnarey of Barra.

A range of glaciated hills, rising from the centre of Lews, and at intervals cut into by the Minch, runs along the east side of the islands Along the west side, washed by the Atlantic, is an irregular plain of sandy soil, locally called Machair.

These islands are called the Outer Hebrides, being the most westerly islands of Scotland, except those of Saint Kilda They form a breakwater against the Atlantic, from Cape Wrath on the north, to Ardnamurchan on the south

The Outer Hebrides were of old called Innse Gall, the Isles of the Gall, the Isles of the Strangers, from the Norse Occupation.

The ancient name of the Long Island, and still traced among the people, was Innis Cat, the Island of the Cat, or Catey Who the Catey were is uncertain, though probably they were the same people who gave the name of Cat Taobh, Cat Side, to Sutherland, and Cat Nis, Cat Ness, to Caithness May not the modern Clan Chatan be of these people? They are called the descendants of the Cat or Catey, and have a cat for their crest

The present inhabitants of the Long Island are essentially Celtic, with some infusion of Norse blood They are a splendid race of people, probably unexcelled, mentally and physically, in the British Isles

The populations of the different islands form an aggregate of over 40,000 souls Of these, forty families occupy about two-thirds of the whole land of the islands, the numerous crofters occupying the other third These crofters retain pastoral and agrestic modes of life, now obsolete elsewhere To describe these modes of life is the object of this paper

All the crofters throughout the Outer Hebrides occupy and work their lands on the Run-Rig System, more or less modified They work under this system in three different modes, two of these being stages of decay An example from each of these three modes will be given from each of three parishes where they are in operation This the writer thinks is preferable to any general description which he could devise These parishes are Barra, South Uist, and North Uist, which form the Southern Division of the Outer Hebrides

Run-Rig

The term Run-Rig seems a modification of the Gaelic, Roinn Ruith—'division run.' In this case the word 'run' is used in the sense of common In Gaelic the System of Run-Rig is usually spoken of as Mor Earann—'great division,' or Mor Fhearann, 'great land' Occasionally, however, an old person calls the system Roinn Ruith This seems the correct designation and the origin of the English term Run-Rig

The system of Run-Rig prevailed of old over the whole British Isles and the Continent of Europe It was common in Ireland, it is extinct in England, and obsolete in Scotland, except to a limited extent in the Western Isles There the system still lives in three different forms, more or less modified—two of these being gradations of decay

Township

The English word Township represents the Gaelic word *Baile*, as applied to a rural locality and to a country community I, however, prefer the word townland to township, having already used it in the paper which Mr Skene asked me to write for his *Celtic Scotland*, and which your Lordship was pleased to commend

The word Baile, townland, often appears in *Origines Parochiales* This invaluable work is a compilation, by Cosmo Innes, from ancient charters and other historical documents affecting the Highlands

The word Baile occurs also in Martin's *Western Isles*, published in 1703 Dr Johnson says that it was this book that gave him a desire to see the Highlands of Scotland, and, therefore, to this book the world is indebted for Johnson's famous *Tour to the Hebrides* A copy of *Martin*, which Johnson and Boswell had with them in the Highlands and Islands, the writer has seen in the Signet Library, Edinburgh

I think the word Townland is recognised by law. I have certainly seen it used in law documents. The townland has a collective existence in various ways,—by tradition, by usage, by the condition of the people, by the consensus of public opinion, and by the treatment of the proprietor I shall endeavour to show this, and in doing so shall confine my observations to the Long Island

Maor.

The word Maor is old, and is used in several languages Before and after the tenth century it carried a territorial title equal to Baron among the Highlanders and to the Jarl of the Norwegians

The name was then applied to the governor of a province, whose office was hereditary, like that of the king. The term Maor is now applied to a petty officer only.

Maor-Gruinnd is a ground officer He is appointed by the Factor—Gaelic, Bailidh—and acts under him On large properties the Maor is practically a sub-factor, and, being the eye, the ear, and the tongue of the Factor in his district, he is often more feared than the factor himself Where the Factor is a non Gaelic speaking man, as has been the case on the Gordon properties, the people look on the Maor with suspicion ' The tongue of the people being then ' in another man's mouth,' as one of themselves graphically said to me, they know not what the Maor says or leaves unsaid concerning them. Nevertheless, there are and have been ground-officers who were far from giving cause for such suspicion, who, on the contrary, devoted their time and energies to the interests of proprietor and people to the neglect of their own Among these have been some of the kindliest men I have ever known

The Constable

There is a Constable (Gaelic, Constabal) in every town, and in some two— one representing the proprietor, the other the people Occasionally the Factor and the crofters elect the Constable conjointly More often, however, the Factor alone appoints the Constable. When this is the case, the crofters murmur that the man thus appointed and paid by the Factor alone is, unconsciously to himself probably, too subservient to the Factor and too remiss in their concerns. For this reason they elect a man to look after their own special affairs

When a Constable is to be elected for the townland, the people meet, and this and all kindred meetings are called Nabac, 'neighbourliness.' If presided over by the Maor the meeting is called Mod, Moot.

If the people meet during the day, they probably meet at a place locally known as Cnoc Na Comhairle—'The Council Hill,' or at Clach Na Comhairle—'The Council Stone.' If they meet at night they meet in some central house on the farm. Almost invariably these meetings are held at night, so as to avoid losing time during the day   The meetings are orderly and interesting

Not infrequently the man proposed for the Constableship by his fellow-crofters of the townland declines the office   Then another is proposed, and perhaps with like result.   Ultimately the people may have to cast lots all round before they get a man among themselves to accept the office, the duties of which are distasteful to them

In some townlands the Constable is elected or re-elected yearly, in some for a term of years, and in others for life

The crofter having been appointed Constable, takes off his shoes and stockings Uncovering his head, he bows reverently low, and promises, in presence of heaven and earth, in presence of God and of men,—Am fianuis uir agus adhair, am fianuis De agus daoine,—that he will be faithful to his trust.   In some places the elected Constable takes up a handful of earth instead of uncovering his feet The object is the same—to emphasise, by bodily contact with the earth, that he is conscious of being made of earth, to which he returns

These and similar simple and impressive customs are disappearing, to the regret of the old people and the antiquary

The services of the Constable appointed by the Factor are paid in money , those of the Constable appointed by the crofters in kind—Fiar am beinn, agus peighinn air machair—grazing on hill and tillage on machair

The duties of the Constable are varied and troublesome—requiring much firmness and judgment   The Constable, however, can always rely upon the assistance of one or all of his fellow-crofters as occasion requires

The peat banks (Gaelic, Staill, Poill of the townland) having become exhausted, the Factor or his Maor marks out a new peat moss

The Constable divides this into the necessary number of stances or haggs, according to the number of tenants in the townland   For these stances the crofters cast lots, as they do for their rigs of land   Lest a man should be placed at any advantage or disadvantage from his neighbours, these stances are again subjected to the lot (Gaelic, Crann), in the course of three, five, seven, or nine years, as the people consider advisable

A peat road (Gaelic, Utraid Moine) has to be made to this new peat moss. Probably the road requires to be made over one, two, or three miles of rock, bog, and moorland.   It is the duty of the Constable to see that every crofter in the townland gives the necessary number of days of free labour, with his horses and carts, spades and pickaxes, to construct this new road

The Constable must see that all the roads of the townland are kept in repair by the mutual co-operation of the crofters , that no unnecessary traffic is carried over these roads during or immediately after wet weather , and that the side and cross drains of the roads run free.

To insure equal distribution of labour these bye-roads are divided into Peighinnean, 'Pennis.' The good and bad, the soft and hard, the steep and level parts of the road are thus divided and allotted   Each crofter must keep his own portion in repair   Should he neglect, he is taken to account by his neighbours, and his portion of road repaired at his expense

The Constable engages the Herdsman and Shepherd of the townland, apportions them ground for potatoes and bere, collects and pays their wages   These wages are self-levied on the crofters according to their rent, as they have a whole croft, a half croft, or a quarter croft

Every townland has a cattle fold on the machair, and another on the gearry— Gaelic, Gearruidh   In wet weather the Constable instructs the Herdsman to keep the cows to the machair, where the fold, from the nature of the soil, is less wet and comfortless to the cows and the women who milk them, than the fold on the gearry

The Constable must see that the dyke enclosing the cattle-fold is repaired in early summer before being used, and that the gate is good and strong—Cadha-Chliadh na Cuithe   The term Cadha-Cliath, literally signifies the gorge or pass wattle.

In wooded districts throughout the Highlands, where materials can be found, doors, gates, partitions, fences, barns, and even dwelling houses, are made of wattle-work

In the case of dwelling houses and their partitions, the wattling is plastered over on both sides with boulder clay, and whitewashed with lime, thereby giving an air of cleanliness and comfort to the house

Of old this wattle-work was largely used by the Celts   It is believed that many of their early houses and churches were made of wattling, and Mr Skene thinks that Saint Columba's first church in Iona was so constructed

One of the Gaelic name of Dublin—Gaelic, Dubhlinne, ' blacklinn'—is Bail-ath-cliath, ' the town of the ford of wattles,' the first bridge over the River Liffey having been constructed of wattle-work

Probably the interlacing so much used and so much admired in ancient Celtic art and sculpturing had its origin in this wattle-work, occasionally called Celtic basket-work

In carting sea-weed up the shore, which is extremely trying upon horses, the Constable sees that no man works his horse too heavily nor too long

When he orders the people to stop work they must stop   In some places there was a latent superstition among the people that the spirits of their horses were in communication with the spirits of heaven   Probably this gave rise to their saying—

' Am fear bhitheas trocaireach ri anam
Cha bhith e mi-throcaireach ri bhruid '

' He who is merciful to his soul
Will not be unmerciful to his beast '

The Constable must see to Cuartachadh a Bhaile, ' rounding the townland '

There being no fences round the fields, there is danger that cattle or horses of their own or neighbouring farms may break loose during night and damage the corn

To guard against this, two of the crofters make a circuit of the townland at night, each two and two of the crofters taking this watching in turns during summer and autumn   This precaution is called Cuartachadh, ' circuiting ' Should the watchers be remiss and damage to result, the two crofters responsible must make good the loss   The damage to the corn being appraised, the two crofters in fault pay it to the Constable, who adds it to the general fund of the townland.   Should cattle or horses from a neighbouring farm cause loss, the owners have to pay the loss. The people are exacting in recovering these valuations 'Is e an cunntas goiṅd, a dh-fhagas an cairdeas fada,' they say It is the short accounting that shall leave the friendship lasting, and they act accordingly.

Those, however, who are thus exacting in pecuniary matters are, nevertheless, kind and considerate to one another in other things Should a crofter or his family be laid up ill, his fellow-crofters help on his work If a man's horse dies, his neighbours bring on his work concurrently with their own, and, if necessary, help him to buy another horse

In connection with their watching, the people speak of a time when they had to kindle fires to scare away wild beasts from their flocks, as they do now in some localities to scare away deer and geese from their crops These fires look picturesque at night, and remind one of Campbell's beautiful poem of the 'Soldier's Dream'—'By the wolf-scaring faggot that guarded the slain'

There is a tradition in Lews of the last wolf slain there, and the place is pointed out Traditions of this nature are elsewhere

I asked the crofters who said that they were in the habit of sitting up at night to watch their corn from deer, if they mentioned this hardship to their Factor 'Yes,' said they, 'but he told us that if we complained to him again he would 'clear us all out of the place, so as to be out of the way of the deer. Therefore, we keep quiet, but suffer'

The Constable buys fresh stock, for the infusion of new blood for his townland, and sells the old He will not allow a crofter to cart sea-weed from the shore till his neighbours have reasonable time to be there, nor will he allow a crofter to cut sea-weed when and where he likes He must see that the Run-Rig land, Imire, of one man is not allowed to lie under water to the injury of the man to whose lot it may fall at next allotting The man must cut a drain to allow the surface water to escape.

Should the crofters of the townland have occasion to complain of a fellow crofter to the Factor, a deputation from the crofters go to the Factor to prefer the complaint The deputation is represented by the Constable alone or in company. The Factor confers with the Constable, giving instructions, and possibly removes the recalcitrant crofter from his holding, should he continue to offend against the customs of the community.

The Constable gives information to the people from the Factor as to days on which the Factor is to collect rents and rates, as to new rules which the Factor wishes enforced, or old ones which he wishes more strictly observed, and various other things.

These are some of the duties devolving on the Farm Constable for the orderly management of the Townland In the past he had to assist the Maor in evicting crofters, sometimes in evicting and pulling down the houses of near and dear relatives

There have been no large evictions in recent years in the Western Islands, nor will there probably be.

Proprietors now visit their properties, taking a kindly interest in their people, and Factors are more considerate One of these, indeed, is a man endowed with more excellency of head and heart, without faults, than ordinarily falls to the lot of man, a man possessing the implicit confidence of proprietors and tenants alike, who daily injures himself to benefit them. Mr John Macdonald, Tacksman, Newton, North Uist, and Factor for Sir John Orde, will not forgive my mentioning his name, but others will throughout the Highlands and Islands, where his name is honoured among all classes

But things were not always so in the Western Isles. Where a factor, in many ways capable and excellent, in those days wished to acquire more land for himself, relations, or friends he seems to have felt no more compunction in destroying the well-being of scores of comfortable crofters, than were they so many sheep   This was the common occurrence of the times.

Nor, incredible as it may seem, was it till years afterwards that some of those absentee proprietors came to know, and that accidentally, of these wholesale removals of scores of their peaceable, loyal, industrious tenants, and of this practical destruction of hundreds of their crofter population

That these and many similar proceedings should have paralysed the whole crofter population of the Western Islands was only natural. Nor does it need a man to live and travel among the islands for a quarter of a century to see and to be convinced that the people of those Western Isles have not yet recovered from the effects of that paralysation

BARRA

The Islands of Barra form an oblong group   Of these islands, eight are inhabited. The Southern Isles of Barra were of old called the Bishop's Isles, because they belonged to the bishop of the see   The head of this wild precipitous chain of islands is still called Bearnaraidh an Easpaig, Bearnarey of the Bishop, occasionally Barra Head—Gaelic, Ceann Bharraidh

The Southern Isles of Barra are famed for birds   These are principally the Puffin, Razorbill, and the Guillemote, Gaelic, Buigire, Dui-eineach, and Langaidh. The Manx Shearwater, Gaelic, Scrab, was extremely abundant there at one time , but since the advent of the Puffin, it is now practically extinct

Both these last are burrowing birds   The Puffin is vicious to a degree, his wonderfully strong, sharp, coulterneb bill cutting keenly as a lance

Of old the crofters of Miuley paid their rents in birds to Macneill of Barra These birds were principally the young of the Shearwater, and called by the people Fachaich, ' fatlings '

The land was divided into crofts called Clitig, Feoirlig, Leth-Pheighinn, and Peighinn.   The Clitig is half the Feoirlig, the Feoirlig is half the Leth-Pheighinn, and Leth-Pheighinn is half the Peighinn, ' Penny '

The Penny Croft paid two barrels, the Halfpenny Croft one barrel, the Farthing Croft one half barrel, and the Clitig Croft one fourth barrel of Fachaichto Macneill

Probably not less than twenty barrels of these birds went to Macneill yearly, and all from the small island of Grianamal, behind Miuley !

The proprietor came over to Miuley a fortnight before, and remained till a fortnight after Lammas Day—Gaelic, La Lunastain   The people were not allowed to go to the rocks till he came , when he left, they had the free range of the cliffs

The people of the Southern Isles do not now kill many birds, being too much occupied otherwise.

The people of Miuley do not seem to have used ropes as they do in Saint Kilda, but to have clambered among the rocks like goats   These rocks are wonderfully grand   Mr Campbell of Islay and the writer measured the highest of these in October 1871, when the barometer showed nearly 800 feet above the sea   The place is named Aonaig, and this particular rock is called Biolacreag. The face of the cliff is as smooth and perpendicular as the wall of a house, and goes sheer down into the Atlantic.

This precipice was the crest of the ancient Macneills of Barra, and ' Biolarecag ' formed the rallying cry of the clan.

XCIX.
—
Alexander
Carmichael

There is probably no more interesting island in Britain than this Island of Miuley, with its wonderful precipices, long narrow sea galleries, several hundred feet high in the perpendicular sides, and marine arcades, winding their gloomy subterraneous ways under the precipitous island.   To boat through these galleries and arcades needs a calm sea, a good crew, and a steady nerve   The writer was the first to discover, and the first and the last to go through much the longest, largest, and gloomiest of these wonderful sinuous sea arcades

The Macneills of Barra lived in a castle on a tidal rock called Ciosmal, in Baile Mhicneill, Macneilltown, now called Castlebay   There are two wells within the walls of this old castle   The people say that the water of these wells comes in pipes under the sea, the pipes being overlaid with large flags

Some fifteen years ago, the then Factor let the castle as a herring-curing station, when the principal well, in the centre of the court, was filled up, and the chapel in the west corner carried away piecemeal as ballast for boats and vessels   The native people, who still fondly cling to the memory of their once proud chiefs, were grieved at the destruction they were powerless to prevent

The site of Ciosmal Castle had been the site of a magazine, wherein the Norsemen kept war materials during the Norse Occupation of the Western Isles

Ciosmal was abandoned by the Macneills during the first quarter of last century   They built houses in three other places, finally settling at Eoligearry, on the north end of the island   The family became extinct in the direct male line in Lieut.-General Roderick Macneill   It is said that so symmetrical in person was General Macneill that ' no eye looked at him without looking at him again '   He was adored by his people, who, with the fidelity of their race, ruined themselves in trying to save him from ruin   They gave him their all

To Dr Macgillivray, the people of Barra are much indebted, and this they gratefully acknowledge   Since he became tacksman of Eoligearry, some forty-four years ago, probably he has given in one form or another some £7000 in work to the people of Barra, while his skill and his medicine are ever at the disposal of all.   The eminent naturalist of that name was brother to Dr Macgillivray.

A curious custom prevails among the people of Barra of apportioning their boats to their fishing banks at sea, much as they apportion their cows to their grazing grounds on land.   The names, positions, extent, characteristics, and capabilities of these banks are as well known to them as those of their crofts

The people meet at church on the 1st day of February—Gaelic, La-Fheill Bride—the Festival of Saint Bridget , and having ascertained among themselves the number of boats engaging in the long line fishing, they assign these boats in proportionate numbers among the banks according to the fishing capabilities of each bank.   The men then draw lots, each head-man drawing the lot for his crew, and thus the boats are assigned to their respective banks for the season.

Should a bank prove unproductive, the boats of that bank are considerately allowed to distribute themselves among the other banks, the boats of which are then at liberty to try the deserted banks   The fishermen say that the ways and migrations of the fishes of the sea are as unaccountable as those of the fowls of the air—here to-day and there to-morrow   They say also that fishes resemble birds in their habits , some fishes, as the Cod and the Conger, in being solitary, like the Raven and the Skua , while some other fishes, as the Saithe and the Herring, are gregarious in their habits, and live in communities, like the Razorbill and the Guillemote.   I am indebted to the intelligent and observant fishermen throughout those islands for much interesting and curious information regarding fishes and sea birds

Having completed their balloting, the fishermen go in to church, accompanied by fathers and mothers, brothers and sisters, wives and children, and sweethearts The good priest says a short service, wherein he commends those 'who 'go down to the sea in ships' to the protection of the holy Saint Barr, after whom Barra is named, of the beautiful Saint Bridget, 'virgin of a thousand 'charms'—'Bride bhoidheach oigh nam mile beus'—on whose festival they are met, of their loved Mother, the golden-haired Virgin, and to the protection, individually and collectively, of the Holy Trinity. The people disperse, chanting—

'Athair, A Mhic, A Spioraid Naoimh,
Biodh an Tri-aon leinn, a la 's a dh-oidhche,
'S air chul nan tonn, no air thaobh nam beann,
Bith'dh ar Mathair leinn 's bith'dh A lamh mu'r ceann
Bith'dh ar Mathair leinn 's bith'dh A lamh mu'r ceann'

Father ! Son ! and Spirit's Might !
Be the Three-in-One with us day and night ,
On the crested wave, when waves run high,
Oh ! Mother ! Mary ! be to us nigh
Oh ! Mother ! Mary ! be to us nigh

Having dispersed, the people repair to their homes, on the way thither eagerly and simultaneously discussing the merits and the demerits of their respective banks To hear their loud and simultaneous talk, one would think that the people were quarrelling But no, this is only their way—the Barra people being peaceable and gentle, and eminently well-mannered and polite

This habit of the Barra fishermen of apportioning their fishing banks may seem antiquated to modern views The fishermen themselves advance good reasons for its retention, some of these being that it prevents overcrowding of boats on the banks, with the consequent entanglement of lines, resulting sometimes in the loss of temper and friendship

In the *Inverness Courier* seventeen years ago, or so, the writer suggested converting the strait between Barra Head and Miuley into a harbour of refuge, by throwing a break-water across the west end A harbour there would be of inestimable benefit to shipping and fishing

Third Stage of Run-Rig.

The arable land of the crofters of Barra is all divided into crofts, no part being in common. The grazing grounds only are held in common, each townland being confined to its own grazing limits The crofters of each townland have their own herdsman, and regulate their own townland affairs with no interference from without.

South Uist

The Island of South Uist forms an oblong, with a range of high hills on one side, and long level low-lying moors and machairs dotted with shallow lakes on the other side The people live on this side In the time of the Clanranalds, the crofters had the hills for their sheep and cattle, and they say that they were very comfortable Since then the greater and best part of the machair has been cleared of crofters, and their townlands converted into large farms, with the whole of the hills added thereto Some of the evicted people were chased among the hills, caught, tied, and shipped like felons to Canada, against which the Canadian press of the day raised a strong protest

The rest of the evicted crofters were thrust in here and there among the other crofters, who were made to share their rocks and morasses with them. And there they are—'Na biasta mora g-itheadh nam biasta beaga, agus na 'biasta beaga deanamh mar a dh fhaodas iad'—The big beasts eating up the little beasts, and the little beasts struggling as best they can—'the survival of 'the fittest'

One acquainted with these islands is struck with the coincidence, possibly accidental, that the large farms are made from the best crofter townlands, while the crofters are huddled together, generally among rocks and bogs No crofters have been removed for the present highly respectable and intelligent tacksmen of the Long Island.

When the crofters had the hills, they migrated to them every summer season with their flocks They remained in the hills till their corn was ripe for shearing when they and their cattle returned to the townland—Gaelic, Baile Apart from the benefit derived by the flocks from the change of grass, the grass 'at 'home' thus left free was of inestimable advantage to the stock during autumn and winter. The stock needed but little house feeding, and that mostly during spring

The crofters say that the change from the malaria of the plains to the bracing air of the hills was of benefit to themselves, and that as a consequence complaints common among them now were then unknown They talk with delight of the benefit they derived in mind, body, and substance from their life among the hills. I entirely agree with them, and believe that these shrewd people are quite equal to their critics

There is one place of which the old people speak with particular favour It is on the Factor's farm of Ormacleit, out at the mouth of Lochaoineart, and at a place called Airi-nam-ban, the 'shealing of the women' There had been a religious house here in the olden times, and from this circumstance the place is named.

These holy sisters had always the good taste to select or get selected for them the best situations for their dwellings This place is no exception One of the many beautiful descriptions of a beautiful place, in the old Gaelic tales, runs thus—

> 'Grianan-aluinn aona chrainn,
> Air chul gaoithe, air aodan greine,
> Far am faicemid an saoghal uile,
> 'S far nach faiceadh duin idir sinn'

> A lovely summer shealing of one tree,
> Behind the wind, in front of the sun,
> Where we could see the world all,
> But where no man could us see

Here the good nuns had such a place to their heart's desire. Behind rises Benmore 2030 feet high, the base of it winding round this beautiful spot, and sheltering it from the west, north, and east In front is the Minch and the sea away as far as the eye can reach beyond Coll and Tiree, dotted with white sails bending in various directions. On the left is Skye, with the snow-capped Coolin Hills, their serrated peaks piercing the ever changing clouds, while ranged away to the south are the hills of Arasaig, Ardnamurchan, and of Mull, in the foreground of which lie, stretched in broken chain, the peaks of the Small Isles and the low-lying Islands of Coll and Tiree Right below this beautiful summer shealing are ivy-clad sea precipices of great height, the home of the king of birds —Righ-nam-Ian, the Golden Eagle The fine anchorage, close below to the right, is the sporting ground of varieties of fish. The bent back of the old man who spoke of this place to me first straightened up; the dim blue eyes, which had seen the changes of ninety-nine years, sparkled with light, and the weak voice trembled with animation as he graphically described the place to me, and the joyous life they lived at the shealing there,

' In life's morning march, when his bosom was young.'

The smoke of the whole people, nuns and all, now ascends through the chimney of a single shepherd.

Highlanders are essentially musical Of old they had songs for all the avocations in which they engaged, particularly for love, war, and the chase Many of these are beautiful—all are chaste They had labour songs, with which they accompanied themselves in rowing, shearing, spinning, fulling, milking, and in grinding at the quern If they sing less now, their silence is due to repression from without.

The tendency of modern cultured life is to have prayers and hymns for special occasions These old people, whom it is the fashion for those who know them least to condemn, had special prayers and special hymns for every occasion

Correctly speaking, the hymns and prayers were one, the prayers being rendered into rhyme to help the memory There was a special prayer on going to sea, a special prayer on going to the shealing, a special prayer for resting the fire at night, for kindling it in the morning, for lying down at night, for rising up in the morning, for taking food, for going in search of sheep, cattle, and of horses. for setting out to travel, and for other occasions

These hymns having been asked for by members of the Commission during their Inquiry, a few are given at the end of this paper

Lying across the north end of South Uist Proper, and separated by a ford nearly a mile wide, is the Island of Benbecula—Beinn-nam-faothla—' hill of the fords ' Stretching out from the south end of the Island, and across the east end of the Sound of Barra, is the rocky island of Eirisgey, whereon Prince Charles landed from France when he came to claim the crown of his fathers in 1745. These Islands are in the parish of South Uist

On a rock above water mark is a sandy knoll whereon he scattered, on landing, the seed of a *Convolvulus major* The seed grew, and the plant has spread over the place The flower is pink, with a mauve tinge, and is very pretty A patriotic gentleman from Harris, Dr Robert Stewart, built a wall round Coilleag a Phrionns, the ' Knoll of the Prince,' as the place is called.

Seven miles north from the south end of South Uist, at Airi-mhuillinn—the ' Mill Shealing'—are the ruins of the house where Flora Macdonald was born In the neighbourhood is a boulder where she met the Prince by appointment when she undertook to take him to Skye Should not these places be marked and held sacred for all time coming ?

Six miles further north is Houbeag, where was born Neill MacEachain, father of Marshal Macdonald, Duke of Tarentum. This tribe of the Macdonalds is locally called Mac Eachain Neill Mac Eachain was the son of a small farmer at Houbeag He had been educated for the priesthood, but did not take orders. He had been schoolmaster for the parish and was acting as tutor in the family of Clanranald, when Lady Clanranald sent him to Skye with Flora Macdonald and her Irish spinning maid ' Betty Burke,' the Prince

Neill Mac Eachain followed the Prince to France, where he changed his name back to Macdonald. He married, and his son entering the army, rose to the rank of Marshal of France and Duke of Tarentum.

In 1825 Marshal Macdonald came to South Uist to see his relations. On coming in sight of the river, near which his father was born, he raised his arm, and exclaimed 'That is the River of Hough   I know it from my father's descrip-'tion.   Many a salmon my father killed there'   On meeting his blind old uncle, he embraced him affectionately, and granted him and his daughter an annuity, and gave to various other relatives sums of money.

He took potatoes with him from the garden his father's father had, and earth from the floor of the house wherein his father was born   This earth was, by his orders, put into his coffin when he died.   He parted with his relatives with many mutual regrets   That was a great day in Houbeag!

Right across the hills from Houbeag, after a two hours' walk, is Corradal, in which is the small cave where Prince Charles lived in hiding, Fo Choill, ' under , the wood,' as the people say, for six weeks   The cave is in the face of a rock on the north side of a narrow glen

Chambers says that about ninety persons knew that the Prince was in Corradal   He might safely have said nine hundred, yet no one attempted to betray him.   The place was full of crofters then, though there are none now within many miles   The Rev John Macaulay, grandfather to Lord Macaulay, was minister in the parish at the time

Intermediate Run-Rig

The low-lying district of Iocar, ' nether,' is a narrow strip lying across from sea to sea on the extreme north end of South Uist   It is bounded on three sides by the sea, and on the fourth by a large farm   This district comprehends nine townlands, and an aggregate of eighty-eight crofters   Each of these crofters has a distinct croft of his own in his townland, and a share in the arable land common to the whole crofters of the district

The crofts of the townlands lie towards the middle of the district.   On the east, between the ragged townlands and the Minch, lies a moor interspersed with rocks, bogs, and water   Where the land is not rock it is heath, where not heath it is bog, where not bog it is black peaty shallow lake, and where not lake it is a sinuous arm of the sea, winding, coiling, and trailing its snake-like forms into every inconceivable shape, and meeting you with all its black slimy mud in the most unexpected places   The crofters of the district send cattle here in spring and early summer, if driven by necessity from want of provender, not otherwise   The moss, particularly at one place, contains much Sundew, *Drosera rotundifolia*, and this the people affirm causes Red Water—Gaelic, Bun Dearg— in their cattle.   The various names the old Highlanders had for this plant indi- cate that they understood its carnivorous nature before Darwin's discovery   The plant was called Lus a Ghadmuin, in reference to its qualities as a hair wash, Lus an Deoghail, from its sucking qualities, and Lus an Dioglaim, from its titillating, tickling nature.   The crofters themselves cultivate no part of this moor, but numerous squatters sent and settled there do

Between the rocky, boggy, water-logged townlands and the Atlantic, is an extensive plain, locally called Machair   This Machair, like the moorland, is held in common by all the crofters of the district   Some portions of the Machair are cultivated, some are under grazing, and much is incapable either of cultivation or grazing, being simply sterile sand

For economic purposes, the eighty-eight crofts of the district are divided into four sections of twenty-two each   These sections or wards are presided over by Constables, and the whole district is presided over by a Maor

The cultivated parts of the Machair are periodically allotted among the eighty-

eight crofters. This is done at Hallowmas—Gaelic, Samhuin. The Scat, Clar, or Leob, as the undivided ground is called, is divided into four quarters

These quarters are ballotted for by the Constables of the Townlands for their respective constituencies. This accomplished, the Constables, aided by the people, the whole supervised by the Maor, subdivide their respective sections into the necessary number of rigs or ridges—Gaelic, Imirean, or Iomairean

The crofters cast lots in their respective wards, and the rig which then falls to a man he retains for three years   At the end of that time the whole cultivation is again let out in grass, and fresh ground broken in as before

During summer and autumn, the flocks of the whole community graze over these Machairs, herded by one or two herdsmen as occasion requires

While each crofter sends more or less stock to the district grazing of the machair, he probably grazes fewer or more cows and horses on the uncultivated portions of his croft at home   These are tethered or tended by a member of the crofter's family

There being no fences in the district of Iocar, except those built by the late Rev Father James Macgrigor, the gaunt cattle and horses of the crofters roam at will when the crops are secured   In their intense struggle for existence, these crofters keep far more stock than their crofts can at all adequately maintain   They do not act upon their own proverb, 'Is fearr aon 'laogh na da chraicionn,' One calf is better than two skins   They give the food to their cattle and horses that they so sorely need for themselves   Considering the quantity and quality of their land, that the cottars living upon them are nearly as numerous as the crofters themselves, while many of these keep nearly as much stock, that practically they support their own poor, and several other considerations that must be taken into account, probably these crofters pay four times the rent paid by the large farms, not that the large farms are under-rented, that as a whole they are not   That the Iocar crofters exist at all is only an evidence of the tenacity of their race   As one of themselves said—'We take a deal of killing, or we would have been killed out long ago'

Of the dykes built by Mr Macgrigor no praise is too good   Mr Macgrigor was the priest of probably the most depressed congregation in Scotland   Yet during his incumbency of over forty years he showed a more admirable example to the people how to improve their crofts than all the proprietors, factors, and tacksmen put together   He built several miles of the most excellent enduring stone dykes round and across his croft, while it is computed that more stone is hid underground in drains made by him than appears in these dykes   And all these stones, together with those that went to build his chapel, chapel-house, and outhouses, Mr Macgrigor quarried from the rocky hillocks and erratic boulders that literally studded the face of the land when he came to the place   This land, so well laid out in parks, is now equal to any in the Western Isles for cropping and grazing

Mr Macgrigor lived on the plainest fare in order to improve his place   He personally superintended the digging and the filling up of every drain, the building of every dyke, and the constructing of every house, while nothing delighted him so much as to see boulders and rocks breaking down before his fire, gunpowder, and crow-bars

The good works that this poor priest accomplished above and below ground, and as a skilful medical man among all denominations, and in social life, are marvellous   Nor are they 'all interred with his bones.' Mr Macgrigor was the last professor in the Catholic College of Lismore   In that island he is still remembered.

Mr Macgrigor was warmly loved and welcomed wherever he went, and nowhere more warmly than by the excellent family of the then minister of the parish, the Rev Roderick Maclean   Mr Maclean, being an excellent classic, as well as an excellent man, read from the Greek and Hebrew Texts to the last. He and Mr Macgrigor were warm friends, and perhaps no more graceful act was ever done by the minister of one denomination to that of another, than was done by the parish minister to the priest   The then factor was depriving Mr Macgrigor of his croft and confiscating his improvements   The minister of the parish, the only man who could do so with safety, used his good offices with the absentee proprietor, and Mr Macgrigor, to the relief of every person, was let alone

A subsequent factor nearly took the place from Mr Macgrigor's successor, not because this lamb himself was accused of disturbing the water, but because, as the factor alleged, erroneously, however, that another lamb of the same kind, in a distant fold, was   Better counsel prevailed, however

These and similar cases show the need of security against arbitrary evictions, at the hands of men whose own despotic will is their law   When men so offenceless, so respected and beloved by the whole community, so narrowly escaped, what chance had obscure crofters who had no one to speak for them ?

What improvements on lands or on houses can be expected under such conditions, and in the absence of proprietors or proprietrixes if misled, however well meaning ?

Dr Alexander Macleod, commonly called An Dotair Ban, from his fair hair, was factor over the South Uist estates for a few years.   During his altogether too brief factorship, Dr Macleod conceived and executed many schemes of great originality and utility for the improvement of the estates   Among other things he placed stones along the strand for growing sea-weed, he planted bent, Gaelic, Muran, over hundreds of acres of sterile sands that are now smiling machairs, and he cut canals—Gaelic, Ligeadh—from lakes to the sea, whereby he drained vast tracts of land hitherto under water   On these canals he placed ingeniously constructed self-acting flood-gates, to let out the fresh and to keep out the salt water

Instead of draining the estates of their money, like others, Dr Macleod endeavoured to drain them of their water, while the many wonderful improvements he effected over these estates testify to his success, and indicate what the estates would have become under his management

When Colonel Gordon of Cluny heard of his death, he wept, though not much given to weeping, and said —'I have had many halflins, but never a whole factor except Dr Macleod'

The people of the Western Isles still speak with admiration of Dr Macleod's head and heart, and of his medical skill.

The people of the Gordon estates had great faith in the ability and integrity of Mr James Drever, now of Orkney, for the improvement of the impoverished estates and people, and they still regret his resignation of the factorship

NORTH UIST.

All the crofter land in North Uist, except that of three farms, is held and worked on the Intermediate System of Run-Rig   This system has been described in South Uist.   The three farms in question are those of Hosta, Caolas Paipil, and Heisgeir   These three are still used and worked entirely on the Run-Rig System, and probably they are the only examples now remaining in Scotland, if not in the British Isles, of this once prevalent System of holding the land and tilling the ground And, perhaps, it is in the fitting order of things that these, the last lingering footsteps of this far-travelled pilgrim from the eye of day, should here sink down on the bosom of endless night, where the last rays of the setting sun sink and disappear in the mysterious fading horizon beyond. But this is a practical age, and these are day dreams. I am no advocate for the retention of a system now effete, and yet I cannot help heaving a sigh of regret on seeing a system, once and for ages, the land system of millions of the human race, now disused, discarded, and disowned, disappearing, and for ever, on the shores of those eerie Western Isles, washed by the Atlantic tide, whose waves pour their dirge-like strains over the dying, while the voice of Celtic Sorrow wails on the lonely ear of Night—

'Cha till, cha till, cha till mi tuille !'

' I return, I return, I return nevermore !'

The townlands of Heisgeir, Caolas Paipil, and Hosta are worked alike. The first contains ten, the second six, and the third four tenants

These three farms were of old occupied by one tenant in each When they were let, one after another, some years ago to small tenants, these new tenants adopted the Run-Rig System in its entirety, as the system best adapted to the circumstances of their position Nor must they be condemned in this without taking all the circumstances of their position into consideration Moreover, these men are probably as well qualified to judge of their own requirements as any person likely to sit in judgment upon them

Heisgeir

Heisgeir is a low-lying sandy island in the Atlantic It is three miles in length, and a mile and a third in breadth at its broadest When the tide is in, the island is divided into three by two fords that cross it, while beyond it lies the Island of Seiley, separated by a strait a third of a mile wide that never dries

Heisgeir lies four and a half miles from North Uist, to which it belongs

The island is variously called Heisgeir, Teisgeir, and Aoisgeir The last form is the key to the meaning of the name, but the first being the most common form I shall adhere to it.

Aoi is a Gaelic name for isthmus An isthmus, Aoi, connected the island of Heisgeir with the mainland of North Uist

The isthmus was called Aoi, as similar places are still called But, partly through the gradual subsidence of the land, and partly owing to the gradual dislodgment of the friable sand forming the isthmus, the isthmus by degrees gave way to fords, and the fords broadened into a strait four and a half miles wide and four fathoms deep Tradition still mentions the names of those who crossed these fords last, and the names of persons drowned in crossing

As the isthmus gradually disappeared, the name Aoi disappeared with it, and became attached to the peninsula beyond it, now an island. A similar process is going on elsewhere, and under precisely similar conditions

And this I take it is the way in which the island of Iona acquired its present Gaelic name This sacred isle is called in Gaelic, I Chalum Chille, and which is usually translated 'Isle of Columba of the Churches' But there is no such word in Gaelic as I for an island. Therefore, I take it that I is simply a mal-pronunciation of Aoi, and that the correct Gaelic name of Iona is, Aoi Chalum Chille. Iona was called Aoi in the year 1088

That Iona became an island as Heisgeir became an island is extremely probable Perhaps there was less subsidence of land, but that a sandy isthmus connected Iona with the opposite shore of Mull must be evident to any person who examines the place at low water

Nor does it militate against this theory that the formation on the Mull side is granite, while that of Iona is gneiss

That the heavy Atlantic surf, ceaselessly beating against a bank of friable sand should ultimately destroy it is only natural   The process is going on at various places along the West Coast   I know men who ploughed and reaped fields now under the sea

The island of Heisgeir is called Heisgeir Nan Cailleach—'Heisgeir of the 'Carlins'   A community of Nuns lived here in connection with Iona   These good Nuns lived there far into Reformation times, and only died out from natural decay   The site of their house was pointed out to me by a lonely old woman who lived on the spot, and who, from her aged appearance, might almost have been the last remaining link between them and us

Divided by a strait a third of a mile wide, and beyond Heisgeir Proper, is Heisgeir Nam Manach—'Heisgeir of the Monks'   The whole extent, rocks included, is half a mile long and half a mile wide   A monastery stood in the olden times where the lighthouse now stands   And I think it is but simple justice to the memory of those good monks of old to believe that they were actuated from pure motives of humanity to build their house on that wild bare bluff to warn passing vessels of their danger.   The lighthouse serves the same purpose now

This is the nearest island to Saint Kilda, and is known to mariners as Monach, but to the natives as Seiley-Seal-isle—Norse   Before the lighthouse was built the island and the rocks around it were much frequented by seals   They have now deserted the place   Shipping is indebted to Mr John Macdonald, Newton, for having drawn the attention of the Lighthouse Commissioners to the need of a lighthouse on this highly dangerous coast.

One summer day long ago, all the men and women in Heisgeir went to Seiley to shear sheep   Having landed their wives on Seiley, the men went to a tidal rock near hand to kill seals   In their hurry to club the seals on the rock they omitted to secure their boat properly, and the boat drifted away before the wind   The women had no boat with which to rescue their husbands, and the tide was flowing rapidly.   The cries of the distressed women were heard by a woman on the opposite side of the strait   End by end this brave woman took down from above water mark a large boat and pulled it across to her agonised sisters   But alas, too late !   The Atlantic waves rose mountains high, as they can rise only round this coast, and the men were swept off the rock one by one and drowned before the eyes of their wives   Some of their wives lost their reason, some their health and strength, and died of broken heart.   Such is the tradition in the place.

The flesh of the seal is called Carr in Gaelic.   This is probably the root of Cardhus—Lent—from Carr-Dhiosg, flesh-weaning, or Carr-Thraisg, flesh-fasting. The flesh of the whale is also called Carr, but the flesh of no land animal is.   It would be curious to trace the cause of this distinction

The people of Uist used to eat seals   One of their proverbs is—

> ' Is math am biadh femanaich
> Aran seagail agus saill roin '

> ' Good food it is for sea-weed worker
> Rye bread and blubber of seal '

The seal blubber was cut into long thin strips.   These were placed on a table

A board, with heavy weight on the top, was placed over the strips of blubber to press out the oil. The people's tastes have changed, and they do not now eat seals. Probably the monks of Monach used seal flesh for their table, and seal oil for their beacon lights

The hapless Lady Grange lived in Heisgeir before she was sent to Saint Kilda.

Run Rig Wholly

All the land in Heisgeir is held in common by all the tenants of the island There are no crofts, and consequently no portion of the land is permanently held by an individual tenant   There are ten tenants, and two of these having two shares each, the land is divided into twelve shares

About Hallowtide—Gaelic, Samhuin—the ten tenants of the island meet for Nabac, 'neighbourliness.' Probably the only thing to be done at the neighbourly conference is to decide upon the piece of ground to be broken up for cultivation This foregone conclusion decided, the men proceed at dawn of day to divide the ground.   The land to be divided is called Scat, Clar, or Leob

The Constable takes a rod and divides the Scat into six equal divisions   At the boundary of each division he cuts a mark—Gaelic, Beum—in the ground, which is called by the curious name of Torc.   The Torc resembles the broad arrow of the Ordnance Department.

The word Torc signifies a notch, and is applied to cattle whose ears are notched These notch-eared cattle—'Torc-Chluasach'—are frequent in the Western Isles, and are spoken of as 'Slioc a Chroidh Mhara,' the descendants of the fabled sea cattle

The Constable, having marked off the Scat or Clar into six divisions, with the willing aid of his fellow-crofters, sends a man out from the people. Probably the man sent out of the way is the herdsman, who has no personal interest in the matter   Each of six men then put a lot—Gaelic, Crann—into a bonnet The man sent out is then recalled, and the bonnet is handed to him. From this the man takes the lots, and places them one after one on a line on the ground   The order in which the lots stand on the ground is the order in which the owners of the lots stand to one another in the shares   Each man knows his own mark, and care is taken when putting them into the bonnet that no two be alike

The two tenants who have double shares, retain their two shares each   The other four tenants subdivide their divisions with the other four men whom they represent   These subdivisions are called, Imirean or Iomairean, rigs or ridges Each two tenants cast lots again for the two subdivided rigs.

These arrangements are carried out quickly and quietly, and as the people themselves correctly say—'Gun ghuth mor gun, droch fhacal'—without a loud voice, without an evil word

The tenants set apart a piece of ground for their herdsman, and this is called in Gaelic, Imir a Bhuachaille, the rig of the herdsman   This is generally the outside ridge bordering on the grazing, and called the 'Imir Ionailt,' the browsing rig   The reason of giving this ridge to the herd is obvious   The man will take care to keep his own ridge safe, and if that ridge be safe the others are sure to be safe, because they lie behind it.

The crofters also set apart pieces of ground for the poor among them   These are called 'Imirean nam boc,' the ridges of the poor, and 'Cianag nam boc'

The kindness of the poor to the poor throughout these islands is wonderful

This arrangement of the land lasts for three years, at the end of which time the ground is let out under grazing as before, and new ground is broken in. This is the Roinn Ruith, Run Rig System, pure and simple

When the townlands are reclaiming moorland, the crofters divide the ground into long narrow strips, about five feet wide In English these narrow strips are called "lazy beds"—why, I do not know In Gaelic they are called Feannag The name is in allusion to the flaying and turning over of the surface This is an admirable way of reclaiming land, especially wet land The deep frequent furrows allow the warmth of the sun to reach the seed in the ground from the top and both sides of the ' bed,' while the drains dry the land The crops produced by this mode of tillage, especially in damp ground, is better than that produced by the plough

The extent of ground which strong bodies of crofters can reclaim in a few years is surprising, and not less so the improved appearance of the land under their operations In this manner vast tracts of country have been reclaimed, and the aspect of nature converted from repulsiveness to attractiveness Too often, however, others than the crofters have reaped the benefit

Long stretches of the west coast of the Outer Hebrides are low and sandy Upon these low-lying sandy shores the Atlantic storms drive great quantities of sea-weed, principally fuci With this fuci the people manure their lands and produce their crops

The people of Saint Kilda sing or used to sing, a joyous song on the arrival of their birds The song begins—

' Bui'cheas dha 'n Ti thaine na Gugachan !
Thaine 's na h-Eoin-Mhora cuideriu '
  Cailin dugh ciaru bo 's a chro '
  Bo dhonn ' bo dhonn ' bo dhonn bheadarrach '
  Bo dhonn a ruin a bhlitheadh am baine dhuit '
  Ho ro ' mo gheallag ' ni gu rodagach '
  Cailin dugh ciaru bo 's a chro—
  Na h-eoin air tighinn ' cluinneam an ceol '

' Thanks to the Being, the Gannets have come,
Yes ' and the Great Auks along with them
  Dark haired girl '—a cow in the fold '
  Brown cow ' brown cow ' brown cow, beloved ho '
  Brown cow ! my love ' the milker of milk to thee '
  Ho ro ' my fair skinned girl—a cow in the fold,
  And the birds have come '—glad sight, I see ' '

In like manner the people of the Outer Hebrides are pleased when they see their wild shores strewn with their thrice welcome sea-weed

In order to apprise them of the arrival of the sea-weed, most farms have a man living near the shore, whose duty it is to hoist a bundle of ragged sea-weed on the top of a pole This man is called Am Peursair, the perchman, and his services are paid in sea-weed and land

Men and girls, with horses and carts and creels, labour assiduously in removing the sea-weed beyond reach of the tide If they did not, perhaps the next tide might sweep the whole away In their eagerness to secure the sea-weed, the people often, with the sea above their knees, work themselves and their horses altogether too much day after day

When sea-weed is abundant on the shore, there is no restriction, but when not abundant, the sea-weed is divided into Peighinnean, ' pennies,' like their land into rigs, ridges

Should other work be pressing, perhaps the landed sea-weed is allowed to lie above the shore for a time If so it soon heats and putrifies, and the smell

XCIX.

Alexander
Carmichael

arising from these innumerable heaps of corruption is strong and offensive to a degree. However, the bountiful ozone from the Atlantic counteracts it all, and no harm arises

If possible, however, the people remove the sea-weed to the ground without delay, and spread it on their fields The people are aware that much of the substance of the sea-weed is thus lost to them But they cannot do better.

Throughout the Long Island the crofters keep stock according to recognised long-established regulations among themselves These vary to some degree in various districts In Lews and Harris the crofters keep stock according to every pound of rent they pay This is called Coir-Sgoraidh, grazing-right Every cow is entitled to her progeny—Bo le h-al But the number of progeny to which a cow is entitled is not the same everywhere. In some districts the cow is entitled to her calf only, in some to her calf and stirk, in some to her calf, stirk, and two-year-old quey, while in some other districts the cow is entitled to her calf, stirk, quey, and three-year-old heifer.

This is called Suim, soum, and a man is entitled to send so many soums to the grazings of his townland A man's whole stock is called Leibhidh, and the amount of stock he is allowed to the grazing of his community is called Suimachadh, souming Of this Leibhidh he sends so many soums to the townland grazing, while he keeps more or less stock of cows and horses at home on his croft In the three townlands of Heisgeir, Hosta, and Caolas Paipil, the tenants are unable to keep any stock at home, being on the Run-Rig system pure and simple The people make what they call a Sumachadh Souming twice a year The first takes place at Bealltain, 1st May, and the second, after the last of the markets are held, when they have sold all the stock they care to sell for the year

In the Uists and Barra the people keep stock according as they have a whole croft, a half croft, or a quarter croft. Each croft in the particular townland is entitled to so many soums

If the stock of a tenant be incomplete it is called Leibhidh Briste, 'Broken Levy' In that case the tenant may dispose of his grazing-right to a neighbour who may have an overstock

The tenants of a townland will not willingly allow a fellow-tenant to sell his grazing outside the townland There are various things which a tenant can do and which he cannot do, and all these things, so intricate to a stranger, so easy to themselves, are well defined

All these stock and land arrangements of the people show that they could not have been devised by fools, nay, that the framers of these regulations must have been shrewd intelligent people

Should a tenant have an overstock of one species of animals and an understock of another species, these species are placed against one another This is called Coilpeachadh, which for want of a better term may be called 'equalizing' In like manner, if a tenant has an overstock of the old and an understock of the young of the same species of animals, the young and the old are placed the one against the other and equalised. After the Coilpeachadh is done, should there still be a balance against the tenant, he must provide for it specially. This is done by buying grass from a neighbour who is short of stock, or from a tenant in a neighbouring townland Or perhaps his fellow-tenants may allow the man to retain the extra cow, horse, heifer, stirk, or sheep, as the case may be, on the grass till he can dispose of it at the market If so, they will exact payment for the grazing, and this payment is added to the general fund of the community towards purchasing fresh stock

In these and all other matters the people are forbearing and considerate towards one another, and a man placed in any difficulty is aided to the utmost by his community If, however, a man is obstinate, he is denounced as Fiacail Gaibhre, gaber tooth, goat tooth, standing out against the customs of the community

XCIX
——
Alexander
Carmichael

The Coilpeachadh varies in some slight degree in some of the islands The following table, however, may be accepted as fairly representing the whole Outer Hebrides .—

1 horse is equal to			8 foals
1	,,	,,	4 one-year-old fillies
1	,,	,,	2 two-year-old fillies
1	,,	,,	{ 1 three-year-old filly { 1 one-year-old filly
1	,,	,,	2 cows
1 cow		,,	8 calves
1	,,	,,	4 stirks
1	,,	,,	2 two-year-old queys
1	,,	,,	{ 1 three-year-old quey { 1 one-year-old stirk
1	,,	,,	8 sheep.
1	,,	,,	12 hoggs
1	,,	,,	16 lambs
1	,,	,,	16 geese

Three one-year-old hoggs are equal to two sheep , one two- ear-old hogg is equal to one sheep, and other modifications

The young of the horse and the cow arrive at maturity at four years of age The old Highlanders never worked nor bred their horses or cattle till they had arrived at maturity They said that the horse, the mare, and the cow lasted twice as long when thus treated In Kintail of old, an entire horse was not allowed to work before he was seven years of age Probably now-a-days that would be considered waiting too long.

The young of most animals are changed to a new name on the first day of winter The foal becomes a Loth or lothag, filly ; the lamb becomes an Othaisg For these things, and for most, if not indeed for all things of this nature, ' the old people' had rhymes to assist the memory These rhymes are invariably expressive and pithy, although now becoming obsolete

The calf changes to a stirk—

' La Samhna theirear gamhna ris na laoigh,
La 'Illeain theirear aidhean riu na dheigh '

At Hallowtide the calf is called a stirk aye,
At Saint John's the stirk becomes a quey

The young are separated from their mothers, and the new name is applied to them at Hallowmas, Gaelic, Samhuin.

Having finished their tillage, the people go early in June to the hill-grazing with their flocks This is a busy day in the townland The people are up and in commotion like bees about to swarm The different families bring their herds together and drive them away The sheep lead, the cattle go next, the younger preceding, and the horses follow. The men carry burdens of sticks, heather-ropes, spades, and other things needed to repair their summer huts (Sgitheil, Bothain) The women carry bedding, meal, dairy and cooking utensils   Round below their waists is a thick woollen cord or leathern strap (Crios-f heile, kilt-band), underneath which their skirts are drawn up to enable them to walk easily over the moors.   Barefooted, bareheaded, comely boys and girls, with gaunt sagacious dogs, flit hither and thither, keeping the herds together as best they can, and every now and then having a neck-and-neck race with some perverse animal trying to run away home   There is much noise   Men—several at a time—give directions and scold.   Women knit their stockings, sing their songs, talk and walk as free and erect as if there were no burdens on their backs nor on their hearts, nor sin nor sorrow in this world of ours, so far as they are concerned   Above this din rise the voices of the various animals being thus unwillingly driven from their homes   Sheep bleat for their lambs, lambs for their mothers , cows low for their calves, and calves low for their dams , mares neigh for their foals, and foals reply as they lightly trip round about, little thinking of coming work and hard fare   All who meet on the way bless the ' Trial,' as this removing is called   They wish the ' Trial ' good luck and prosperity, and a good flitting day, and, having invoked the care of Israel's Shepherd on man and beast, they pass on

When the grazing-ground has been reached and the burdens are laid down, the huts are repaired outwardly and inwardly, the fires are rekindled, and food is prepared   The people bring forward their stock, every man's stock separately, and, as they are being driven into the enclosure, the constable and another man at either side of the gateway see that only the proper souming has been brought to the grazing   This precaution over, the cattle are turned out to graze.

Having seen to their cattle and sorted their shealings, the people repair to their removing feast, Feisd na h-imrig , or shealing feast, Feisd na h-airidh   The feast is simple enough, the chief thing being a cheese, which every housewife is careful to provide for the occasion from last year's produce   The cheese is shared among neighbours and friends, as they wish themselves and cattle luck and prosperity

> Laoigh bhailgionn bhoirionn air gach fireach,
> Piseach crodh na h-airidh

Every head is uncovered, every knee is bowed, as they dedicate themselves and their flocks to the care of Israel's Shepherd.

In Barra, South Uist, and Benbecula, the Roman Catholic faith predominates , here, in their touching dedicatory old hymn, the people invoke, with the aid of the Trinity, that of the angel with the cornered shield and flaming sword, Saint Michael, the patron saint of their horses , of Saint Columba the holy, the guardian over their cattle , and of the golden-haired Virgin Shepherdess, and Mother of the Lamb without spot or blemish.

I.

> ' A Mhicheil mhin ' nan steud geala,
> A choisin cios air Dragon fala,
> Air ghaol Dia' us Mhic Muire,
> Sgaoil do sgiath oirnn dian sinn uile,
> Sgaoil do sgiath oirnn dian sinn uile

II

> ' A Mhoire ghradhach ' Mathair Uain-ghil,
> Cobhair oirnne, O.gh na h-uaisle,
> A rioghainn uai'reach ' a bhuachaille nan tredu !

Cum ar cuallach cuartaich sinn le cheil,
Cum ar cuallach cuartaich sinn le cheil

III

'A Chalum-Chille! chairdeil, chaoimh,
An ainm Athar, Mic, 'us Spioraid Naoimh,
Trid na Trithinn ! trid na Triath !
Comraig sinne, gleidh ar trial,
Comraig sinne, gleidh ar trial

IV

'Athair ! A Mhic ! A Spioraid Naoimh !
Bi'eadh an Tri-Aon leinn a la's a dh-oidhche !
'S air machair loim, no air rinn nam, beann,
Bi'dh an Tri-Aon leinn 's bith A lamh mu'r ceann,
Bi'dh an Tri-Aon leinn, 's bi'th A lamh mu'r ceann '

Iasgairean Bharraidh—

'Athair ! A Mhic ! A Spioraid Naoimh !
Bi'eadh an Tri-Aon leinn, a la 's a dh-oidhche !
'S air chul nan tonn, no air thaobh nam beann,
Bi'dh ar Mathair leinn, 's bith A lamh fo'r ceann,
Bi'dh ar Mathair leinn, 's bith A lamh fo'r ceann

The Shealing Hymn

I

'Thou gentle Michael of the white steed,
Who subdued the Dragon of blood,
For love of God and of Mary's Son
Spread over us thy wing, shield us all !
Spread over us thy wing, shield us all !

II.

'Mary beloved ! Mother of the White Lamb,
Protect us, thou Virgin of nobleness,
Queen of beauty ! Shepherdess of the flocks !
Keep our cattle, surround us together,
Keep our cattle, surround us together

III

'Thou Columba, the friendly, the kind,
In name of the Father, the Son, and the Spirit Holy,
Through the Three-in-One, through the Three,
Encompass us, guard our procession,
Encompass us, guard our procession.

IV

'Thou Father ! Thou Son ! Thou Spirit Holy !
Be the Three-One with us day and night,
On the machair plain, on the mountain ridge,
The Three-One is with us, with His arm around our head,
The Three-One is with us with His arm around our head.

Barra Boatmen's Version of last Verse—

'Thou Father! thou Son! thou Spirit Holy!'
Be the Three-One with us day and night,
And on the crested wave, or on the mountain side,
Our Mother is there, and Her arm is under our head,
Our Mother is there, and Her arm is under our head'

In North Uist, Harris, and Lews, the Protestant faith entirely prevails, and the people confine their invocation to,

> The Shepherd that keeps Israel,
> He slumbereth not nor sleepeth
>
> Feuch air Fear Coimhead Israeil,
> Codal cha'n aom no suain

As the people sing their dedication, their voices resound from their shealings here literally in the wilderness, and as the music floats on the air, and echoes among the rocks, hills, and glens, and is wafted over fresh-water lakes and sea-lochs, the effect is very striking

The walls of the shealings in which the people live are of turf, the roof of sticks covered with divots There are usually two shealings together, the larger the dwelling, the smaller the dairy This style of hut (Sgithol) is called 'Airidh' or shealing, and 'Both cheap,' or 'Bothan cheap,' turf bothy, to distinguish it from the 'Both cloiche' or 'Bothan cloiche,' stone bothy. This is entirely constructed of stone, the roof tapering to a cone more or less pointed. The apex of the cone roof is probably finished off with a flag, through the centre of which there is a hole like that through an upper millstone, the opening for the egress of smoke and the ingress of light There is a low door-way with a removable door, seldom used, made of wicker work, wattles, heather, or bent In the walls of the hut, two, three, or four feet from the floor, are recesses—Gaelic, Buthailt, Scottish 'bole'—for the various utensils in use by the people, while in the bosom of the thick wall low down near the ground are the dormitories wherein the people sleep The entrance to these dormitories, slightly raised above the floor, is a small hole, barely capable of admitting a person to creep through This sleeping place is called 'Crupa, from 'Crupadh,' to crouch It was a special feature in the architecture of the former houses of St Kilda, the houses themselves being called 'Crupa' from this characteristic. These beehive stone houses are still the shealings of the Lews people Some are also to be seen in the forest of Harris, but none in either of the Uists or in Barra. In these places the people have practically ceased going to the summer shealings Invariably two or three strong healthy girls share the same shealing Here they remain making butter and cheese till the corn is ripe for shearing, when they and their cattle return home The people enjoy this life at the hill pasturage, and many of the best lyric songs in their language are in praise of the loved summer shealing *

Considerable changes are now taking place among the people of the Outer Hebrides as to the rearing and the disposing of stock Markets are more open to them, and they can sell their stock early, and of this they take advantage But under their old conditions, and considering all their circumstances, which must be weighed before judging, probably none better than their old systems were ever devised

---

* The writer has a small primitive stool, upon which Prince Charlie sat in one of these summer shealings during his wanderings after the disasters of Culloden The people spoke and sung of the Prince as, Am Buachaille Ban, Am Buachaille Buidhe, 'the fair-haired 'Herdsman,' 'the yellow-haired Herdsman' The allusion was understood without committing themselves

In various localities and on various occasions I made minute inquiries of old people as to the detailed farm stock and domestic substance of their fathers The people then had more land and of better quality , they had more horses, sheep, and cattle ; they had more crop, and of better quality , they had better nourishing food, and they had better bed and body clothing They had also more constructive ingenuity in arts and manufactures, and they had more mental and physical stamina, and more refinement of manners

Therefore, go back to the old order of things under improved conditions Unloosen their cords, and allow the people to expand by filling up the central rungs in the land ladder, all of which are at present absent, rendering it impossible for a crofter, however industrious, to rise higher than he is To my thinking it is impolitic, as well as unjust, to hem the people into a corner, thereby impoverishing the many to enrich the few The people of the Outer Hebrides are admirable workers by sea and land, and if they are less persevering than they might be, it is the fault of circumstances

XCIX.
— —
Alexander
Carmichael

Old Hymns

The oral lore of the old Highland people is rapidly dying out with the old people themselves There is an essential difference between the old and the young people The young people are acquiring a smattering of school education in which they are taught to ignore the oral literature which tended to elevate and ennoble their fathers. In his anxiety to rescue what he could of this unwritten literature of various kinds, the writer has sacrificed promotion several times offered to him A few hymns from this mass of old lore are given in this paper at the desire of the noble Chairman of this Commission, Lord Napier and Ettrick

XCIX
—
Alexander
Carmichael

URNUIGH SMALAIDH AN TEINE.—PRAYER ON 'SMOORING' the FIRE

The following beautiful little prayer is said by women in South Uist while putting up their fire for the night   And the people believe that those mentioned in the prayer do watch over themselves and their households and shield them from harm while they sleep

> ' Kind hearts are more than coronets,
> And *simple faith* than Norman blood '

The Scotch word 'Smooring,' smothering, is the nearest equivalent of the Gaelic word Smaladh that occurs to me

> ' Tha mi smaladh an teine,
> Mar a smalas Mac Moire
> Gu mu slan dha'n taigh 's dha'n teine,
> Gu mu slan dha'n chuideac uile
> Co siod air a lar ? Peadair agus Pal,
> Co air a bhi'eas an fhaire noc ?
> 'Air Moire mhin-gheal 's air a Mac
> Beul De a thuradh, aingeal De a labhradh
> Aingeal an dorus gach taighe,
> Ga'r comhnadh's ga'r gleidheadh,
> Gu'n tig la geal a maireach '

Translation—

> I smoor the fire,
> As it is smoored by the Son of Mary
> Blest be the house, blest be the fire,
> And blessed be the people all
> Who are those on the floor ? Peter and Paul
> Upon whom devolves the watching this night ?
> Upon fair gentle Mary and her Son
> The mouth of God said, the angel of God tells
> An angel in the door of every house,
> To shield and to protect us all,
> Till bright day-light comes in the morning

AN T ALTACHADH LEAPA —THE BED BLESSING

The following prayer is said or sung by Catholics in South Uist, in going to bed   The old man from whom I first took it down, told me that he said it every night since he was fifteen years of age, and that it had been taught him by his father

I

> Tha mise laidhith noc, le Moire 's le' Mac,
> Le Mathair mo Righ, tha ga-m' dhion o gach loc,
> Cha laidh mi luis an olc, cha laidh an t-olc liom,
> Ach la'idh mi le Dia, 'us la'idh Dia liom

II

> Lamh dheas De fo m'cheann,
> Suillse an Spioraid os mo chionn ,
> Crois nan naogh aingeal tharam sios,
> O mhullach mo chinn gu iocar mo bhonn.

III

XCIX.

Alexander
Carmichael.

.   .   :   .   .   .   .
.   .   .
Crois Mhoire 's Mhicheil, ma-rium ann an sith,
M' anam a bhi 'm firinn, gu'n mhi-run am chom.

IV

O Ios gu'n loc, a cheusadh goirt,
Fo bhinn nan olc a sgiursadh Thu ;
A liuthad loc, a rinn mo chorp,
Nach faod mi noc a chunntachadh (1)

V

A Righ na Fola Firinnich,
Na dibir mi o d' mhuinntireas ;
Na tagair orm mo mhi-cheartan ;
Na di-chuimhnuich ad' chunntadh mi (1)

VI

Guidheam Peadair, guidheam Paul,
Guidheam Moir Oigh agus a Mac,
Guidheam an da ostal deug,
Gu'n mise dhol eug a noc

VII

A Dhia agus a Mhoire na glorach,
Ios a Mhic na h-Oighe cubhraidh,
Cumaibh sinne o na piantaibh ,
{ 'S o'n teine dhorcha dhuinte.
{ 'S o'n teine shiorraidh mhuchta

VIII

.   .   .   .   .   .
.   .   .
M anam aig fear shorchar na frithe (2)
Michal Geal an codhail m' anama

(1) The IV. and V verses were not in the first version I obtained of this beautiful hymn   I am not sure that they originally formed part of it   This, however, can only be a matter of conjecture.   Not infrequently in old Gaelic poetry, sacred and profane, the measure, rhyme, assonance, and even subject, change in the same poem   Old English poetry is the same

(2) I am not satisfied that I have correctly translated this line   *Sorch* means "light," in contradistinction to *dorch* "dark "   *Sorchar*, I take it, is the man or being of light, as *dorchar* is the man or being of darkness   *Sorch*, "Light," is the name of a woman in the Long Island.   A C

The Bed Blessing —Close Translation

I

I lie down this night, with Mary and with her Son,
With the Mother of my King, who shields me from harm ,
I shall not lie down with evil, nor shall evil lie down with me,
But I shall lie with God, and God will lie down with me

XCIX

Alexander
Carmichael

II.

The right hand of God under my head,
The light of the Spirit Holy shining over me,
The cross of the nine angels along me, down
From the crown of my head to the soles of my feet

III.

.   .   .   .

.   .   .   .

Be the cross of Mary and of Michael with me in peace,
May my soul dwell in truth, and my heart be free of guile

IV

O Jesus without offence that wast crucified cruelly
Under sentence of the evil ones, Thou wert scourged,
The many evils done by me in this body
That cannot this night be numbered!

V

Thou King of the Blood of Truth,
Omit me not from thy covenant,
Exact not from me for my sins,
Nor forget me in thy numbering

VI.

I pray Peter, pray I Paul.
I pray Mary, Virgin, and her Son,
I pray the Apostles twelve
That I may not die this night.

VII

Oh, God!   Oh, Mary of Glory!
Oh, Jesus! Thou Son of the Virgin fragrant,
Keep ye us from the pains,
{ And from the dark hidden fire,
{ And from the everlasting suffocating fire

VIII

.   .   .   .

.   .   .

My soul is with the Light of the mountains,
Archangel Michael shield my soul!

BEANNACHADH BUACHAILLEAC.—THE HERDING BLESSING

This invocation used to be sung by old men and women while tending their cattle among the hills of South Uist.

I

Cuireamsadh an spreidh so romham,
Mar a dh-orduich Righ an domhan
Moire ga'n gleidheadh, ga'm feitheadh, ga'n coimhead,
Air bheann, air ghleann, air chomhnart,
Air bheann, air ghleann, air chomhnart.

II

Eirich a Bhride mhin-gheal,
Glacsa do chir agus d'fholt,
O rinn thu daibh eolas gu'n aura
Ga'n cumail o chall 's o loc,
Ga'n cumail o chall 's o loc.

III

O chreag, o chabhan, o allt,
O chara cam, o mhille sluic,
O shaighde nam ban seanga sith,
O chridhe mhi-ruin, o shuil an uilc,
O chridhe mhi-ruin, o shuil an uilc

IV

A Mhoire Mhathair ! cuallaichs an t-al gu leir !
A Bhride nam basa-mine, dionsa mo spreidh !
A Chalum chaoimh, a naoimh is fearr buadh,
Comraig-sa crodh an ail, bairig am buar,
Comraig-sa crodh an ail, bairig am buar

THE HERDING BLESSING —CLOSE TRANSLATION.

I

I place this flock before me,
As 'twas ordered by the King of the world,
Mary Virgin to keep them, to wait them, to watch them,
On ben, on glen, on plain,
On ben, on glen, on plain

II

Arise thee, Bridget, the gentle, the fair,
Take in thine hand thy comb and thy hair ;
Since thou to them madest the charm,
To keep them from straying, to save them from harm,
To keep them from straying, to save them from harm

III.

From rocks, from snow-wreaths, from streams,
From crooked ways, from destructive pits,
From the arrows of the slim fairy women,
From the heart of envy, from the eye of evil,
From the heart of envy, from the eye of evil

IV

Mary Mother ! tend thou the offspring all,
Bridget of the white palms ! shield thou my flocks,
Columba, beloved ! thou saint of best virtues,
Encompass the breeding cattle, bestow thy protection on the herds
Encompass the breeding cattle, bestow thy protection on the herds.

Alexander
Carmichael

XCIX.

RANN BUACHAILLEAC—THE HERDING RUNE.

This parting blessing used to be sung by old people in South Uist when sending their cattle away to the pastures in the morning

I

Siubhal beinne, siubhal baile,
Siubhal gu re fada farsuinn,
Buachaille Mhic De m'ar casaibh,
Gu mu slan a thig sibh dachaidh,
 Buachaille Mhic De m'ar casaibh,
 Gu mu slan a thig sibh dachaidh.

II

Comraig Dhia agus Chalum-Chille,
Bluth m'ar timchioll a fabh 's a tilleadh,
Agus Banachaig nam basa-min-gheal,
Bride nan or-chiabh donn !
 Agus Banachaig nan basa min-gheal,
 Bride nan or-chiabh donn !

HERDING RUNE —CLOSE TRANSLATION ADDRESSED TO THE CATTLE.

I

Travel ye moorland, travel ye townland,
Travel ye gently far and wide,
 God's Son be the Herdsman about your feet,
 Whole may ye home return
  God's Son be the Herdsman about your feet,
  Whole may ye home return

II.

The protection of God and of Columba,
Encompass your going and coming,
 And about you be the milkmaid of the smooth white palms,
 Bridget of the clustering hair, golden brown
  And about you be the milkmaid of the smooth white palms,
  Bridget of the clustering hair, golden brown !

TALADH NAM BANACHAG —THE LULLABIES OF THE MILKMAIDS

These lullabies are sung by the milkmaids of Uist to soothe their cows They are varied in tone and measure, while not unfrequently these change in the same song to suit the different actions of milking

The cows become so accustomed to these milking lilts that they will not give their milk without them, nor, occasionally, without their own favourite airs. Hence a milkmaid

'Who has no music in her soul'

succeeds but indifferently among a fold of Highland cows Owners of stock prefer as milkmaids those who are possessed of some voice and 'go' to please the cows, this being to them a matter of considerable importance.

BANACHAIG NAM BO—THE MILKMAID OF THE COWS   XCIX

The following air, one of many, is sung by milkmaids in South Uist as they   Alexander
milk their cows.   Carmichael.

I.

O m' adhan ! bo m' adh min !
M' adhan cri', coir, gradhach,
An' ainm an Ard-Righ,
     Gabh ri d' laogh (1) !

II

An' oidhche bha am Buachaille muigh,
Cha deachaidh buarach air boin,
Cha deachaidh geum a beul laoigh,
     A caoineadh Buachaille chruidh !

III

Thig a Mhoire 'us blith a bho,
Thig a Bhride 's comraig i,
Thig a Chalum Chille chaoimh,
     'Us iadh do dha laimh mu m' bhoin !

IV

Mo bho lurach dhugh, bo na h-airidh,
Bo a bhathaiche ! mathair laogh !
Luban siamain air crodh na tire,
     Buarach shiod air m' adhan gaoil !

V

'Sa bho dhugh sin ! 's a bho dhugh !
'S ionan galar domhs 'us duits—
Thus a caoidh do cheud laoigh caoin,
     Mise 'us m' aona mhac gaoil fo'n mhuir !
     Mise 'us m' aona mhac gaoil fo'n mhuir !

(1) Occasionally a calf dies, and the mother cow is restive, and will not give the milk. To quiet her, and obtain her milk from her, the skin of her dead calf is placed on a skeleton frame calf, made for the purpose This is placed before the cow, and the deception has the desired effect The skin, however, must be that of the cow's own calf. That of another cow's calf, however much like her own in colour and size, is disdainfully tossed aside and kicked away by the cow

In wooded districts, where rods are got, the frame calf is made of wickerwork. This sham calf is variously called Laoicionn, Loircean, Lulagan, Tulgan, and Tulachan The first two names refer to the skin and appearance of the sham calf, while the last three names refer to the rocking, fretting motion of the calf when sucking under its mother A boy near moves the tulachan now and again, to make the cow believe that all is right, while the maid is busy the while taking away the milk from the pleased cow ! This is the origin of the term 'tulchan,' as applied to a bishop who draws the stipend but does not perform the work of a bishop—a term sufficiently known in Scottish ecclesiastical history.

XCIX.
—
Alexander
Carmichael

THE MILKING SONG —CLOSE TRANSLATION.

I

O ! my heifer, ho ! my gentle heifer,
My heifer so full of heart, generous and kind
In the name of the High King,
    Take to thy calf (1)

II

That night the Herdsman was out,
No shackle went on a cow,
Nor ceased a low from a calf,
    Wailing the Herdsman of the flock

III

Come Mary (Virgin) and milk the cow ,
Come Bridget and encompass her ,
Come Culum Cille, the beneficent,
    And wind thine arms around my cow

IV

My lovely black cow, thou pride of the shealing !
First cow of the byre, choicest mother of calves !
Wisps of straw round other cows of the town land,
    But a shackle of silk on my heifer so loved

V.

Thou black cow mine ! own gentle black cow !
The same disease afflicts thee and me ,
Thou art grieving for thy beautiful first calf !
    And I for mine only beloved son under the sea !
    And I for my only beloved son under the sea !

' One touch of Nature makes the whole world akin '

TALADH NA BANACHAIG —THE MILKMAID'S LULLABY

The following poem is interesting from the three chiefs introduced at the end. Although these lilts were meant only to soothe and quiet the cows in being milked, they yet show, unconsciously, much that is interesting of the past, if not of the present, life of the Highlands and Islands.

    Fonn —Ho m' adhan ! ho m' adh min !
           Ho m' adhan ! ho m' adh min !
           Ho m' adhan ! ho m' adh min !
           A chrigheag chri, is toigh lom thu

    Fhaic thu bho ud air an liana,
    'S a laogh mear aic air a bialaobh
    Dean thusa mar a rinn i chiana
        Thoir am bain a laoigh na Fianaich
           Ho m' adhan, &c

II.

Thoir am baine bho dhonn !
Thoir am baine gu trom 's gu torrach,
Thoir am baine bho dhonn,
    'S na h-uaislean a tigh'nn an bhaile
      Ho m' adhan, &c

III

Thoir am baine bho dhonn !
'S gu'n ann daibh ach an t-aran !
Thoir am baine bho dhonn,—
    Macneill ! Macleoid ! MacAilean !
      Ho m' adhan

THE MILKMAID'S LULLABY —CLOSE TRANSLATION

Chorus —Ho my heifer ! ho my heifer fair !
    Ho my heifer ! ho my heifer fair !
    Ho my heifer ! ho my heifer fair !
    Thou heartling, heart I love thee !

I

Behold that cow on the plain,
With her frisky calf before her ;
Do thou as she did a while ago—
    Give thy milk thou calf of Fianach
      Ho my heifer, ho my heifer fair.

II

Give thy milk brown cow,
Give thy milk so abundant and rich,
Give thy milk brown cow,
    And the gentles coming to the townland.
      Ho my heifer, &c

III

Give thy milk brown cow,
And that there is nothing for them but bread
Give thy milk brown cow,
    Macneill ! Macleod ! Clanranald !
      Ho my heifer, &c

MAR CHIREIN NAN STUAGH

The following verses are said to have been composed in Benbecula in the time of bows and arrows. They are singularly chaste, beautiful, and elevated They indicate, I think, the wonderful natural refinement of the people who could appreciate, preserve, and repeat these, and whole libraries of similar oral literature, throughout the past ages.

The oral literature of the Highlands and Islands is singularly pure in tone and poetical in expression I have taken down large quantities of this literature, probably a small library in the mass, and I have never heard, either in this or among the people, an unbecoming word or an impure story

2 h

XCIX
—
Alexander
Carmichael

I went much among the very poorest of the people, among a people whose pinched features betrayed their poverty, yet during nearly seventeen years in Uist I was never once asked for charity   Their proprietor in South Uist, the late Mr John Gordon, did not exaggerate when he said—' The Uist people are all born gentlemen—every man of them'   Yet, these are the people so often misrepresented, and sometimes so cruelly maligned by men who do not know them

The Uist people are excellent workers, and for the farming best adapted for their country infinitely before the best farming representatives that have been brought against them from the south   All these successively have had to adopt the native system of farming, after proving the unsuitableness of their own

I.

Mar chirein nan stuagh uaine, ta mo ghaol,
A h-eugasg tlath, mar dhearsa speuran ard ,
Mar sheudan loinneircach, a da shuil chaoin ,
Mar arradh air bharr sleibh, fo ghrein nan trath

II

O ' càit am facas bean is aille snuagh,
Cà'm facas riabh air cluain, le ceumaibh sèimh,
Do shamhuil fein, a gheug nam mile buadh,
Mar chlacha, a buadha, 'san or is aille sgèimh '

In the following translation I have endeavoured to adhere closely to the original

THE WHITE CREST OF THE WAVE

I

To the white crest, of the green wave, I liken my love,
Her countenance warm, like the beaming sky above .
Like brilliant jewels, are her two blue sparkling eyes,
Like the glancing sunbeams, all radiant from the skies

II

Oh ' where has e'er been seen, a lovelier form or face ?
On lawn, or plain, or field, of statelier mien or grace ?
Thou branch of thousand beauties, in thy pride of beauty's joy,
Thou gem in purest gold, yea, gold without alloy '

.

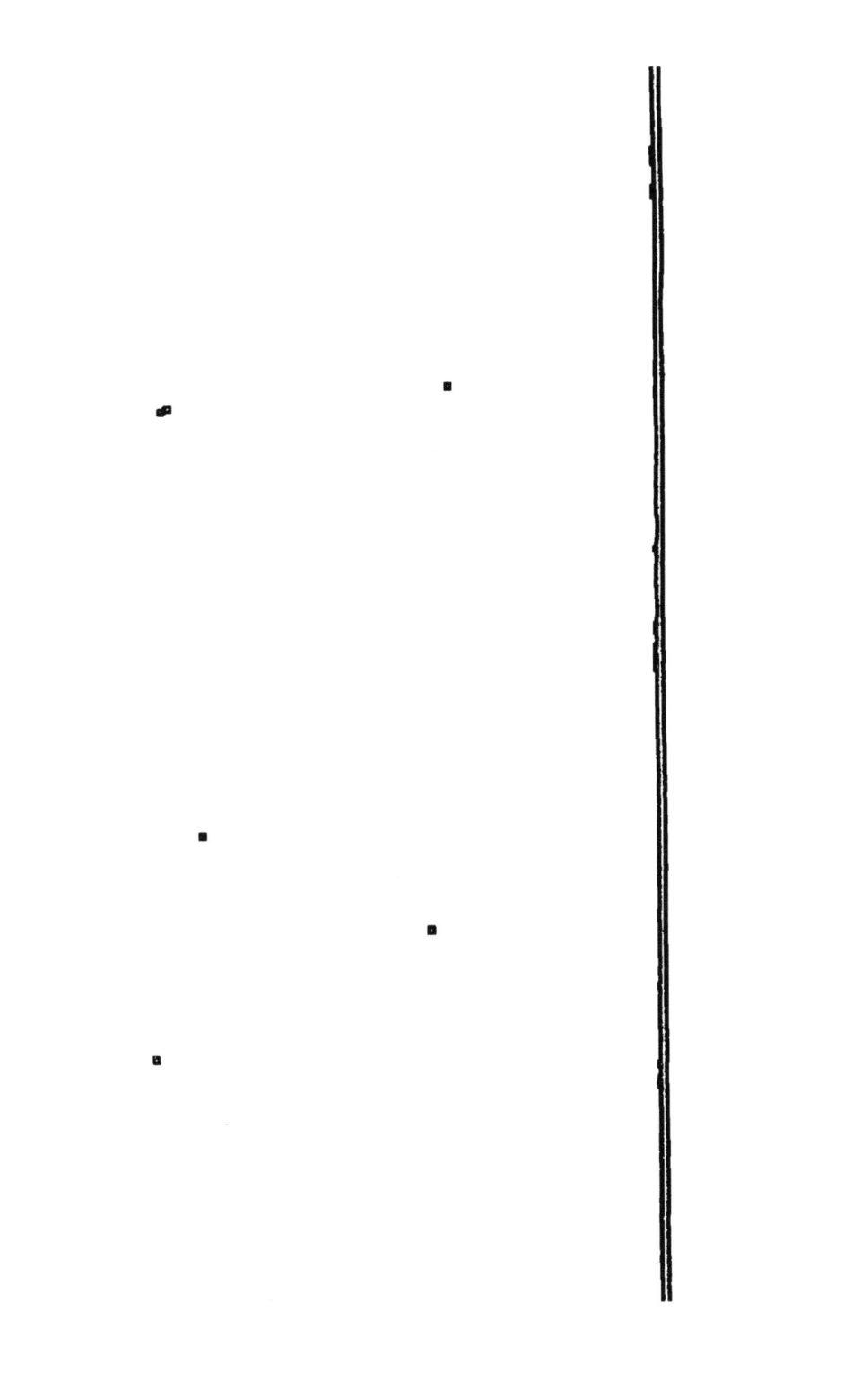

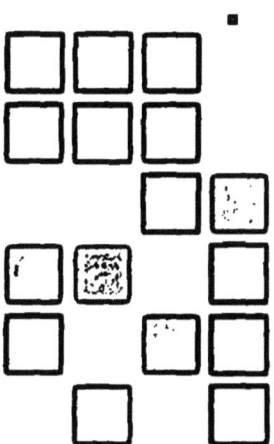